Reap The Wild Wind

Selected Poems by Juliana Byers

Juliana Byers

BookLeaf Publishing
India | USA | UK

Reap The Wild Wind

Selected Poems by Juliana Byers

© 2021 Juliana Byers

Presentation by *BookLeaf Publishing*

Web: www.bookleafpub.com

E-mail: info@bookleafpub.com

ISBN: 9789358361513

First edition 2021

For the Fanstory community, who loved every word

For Grandma

I scattered flowers on the shore

And spoke a softly whispered prayer

That you'll be here forevermore

I scattered flowers on the shore

But should you knock on heaven's door

I will not hold you here, I swear

I scattered flowers on the shore

And spoke a softly whispered prayer

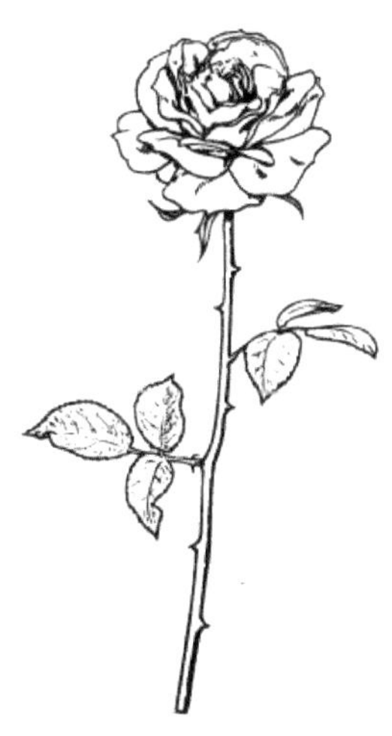

In Dark Places

I've languished long in dripping caves

No sun, nor stars to count the days

No company but shadows cold

Suffocating in midnight's fold

But in the dark, there's light, they say

With light, there's reason to be brave

Throw off the yoke of terror's hold

He'll not stand long if you are bold

So have no fear, let dreams abound

For in dark places, gold is found

Drifting With Death

I've heard a tale in the night

About four wandering galleys

They're crewed by men all dead of blight

I've heard a tale in the night

Of men who had nowhere for flight

And the death they brought, no tally

I've heard a tale in the night

About four wandering galleys.

Silent Devotion

Do I love you? No.

This singular expression

Imprecise in its nature

Bland upon the tongue

Would do you an injustice

For we so often toss it

Frivolously, carelessly

Upon the least deserving

That which is material

Replaceable by nature

So do forgive me

In announcing this one truth

That devotion such as mine

Inexpressible

Is better said by silence

Reap The Wild Wind

If mortals fear but one dread thing

It's Reaper's fearsome scythe

The rustle of his haunting cloak

His scratching in the night

He counts upon his abacus

The souls he has accrued

Cold mortal shades fill Reaper's halls

But this he'll never do.

He'll never reap the wild wind

Nor still the raging seas

The icy blizzard never touch

Nor the storm bring to her knees

No more darken golden sunshine

Than shatter crystal dew

He cannot take from springtime grace

Nor autumn's marvellous hues

So, while mortals fall before him
The Earth stands tall and proud
For she knows he'll never take her
Beneath his gloomy shroud

In Children's Gardens

In children's gardens fairies play,

While sunlight dances on their wings,

Their laughter sounds throughout the day,

In children's gardens fairies play.

When people come they shy away,

Sent running from their fairy rings,

In children's gardens fairies play,

While sunlight dances on their wings.

When Arthur Married Guinevere

When Arthur married Guinevere

Camelot gave a rousing cheer

For this great beauty, sweet and fair

Sat enthroned on the golden chair

Wise Merlin never dreamed he'd fear

When Arthur married Guinevere

But looking towards the blessed pair

He felt a slight chill stir the air

From afar wicked Morgan glared

A cruel breeze pulling at her hair

When Arthur married Guinevere

She knew not how to interfere

Their wedding was a grand affair

At the queen none could help but stare

Oh, who knew that the end was near

When Arthur married Guinevere

When Children Smile

Sometimes the world is bright and gay

And all's well with each passing day

Under blue skies, green fields rest

Song bursts from birds with feathered

breasts

But sometimes it all turns to grey

And raindrops fall where sunbeams played

Nature cowers, and thunders roars

But in these times, just stop and pause

Remember...

If things have been grey a while

Rainbows come when children smile

Immortality

Of death only the immortal know,

The true pain and sorrow when loved ones

go. When Fate comes with deceptive calm,

And tears our dear ones from our arms.

Now lonely days as long as years,

Torture forever without a care.

The nights are silent, the skies are grey,

I'll suffer forever and a day.

So who wants to live for eternity,

When I can't have you and you can't have me?

The Silent Stillness

Despite the silent stillness

When all my life was grey

Though each road wound in circles

To Him I could not pray

And in that silent stillness

That seemed to mark the end

Wicked, twisting dark closed in

I could not find a friend

For with that silent stillness

A thought I'd always feared

Slithered in my consciousness

Said 'God was never here'

But in the silent stillness

I thought I saw a light

Sent the demon cowering

And chased away the night

Now in the silent stillness

I saw that I'd been wrong

I'd never been abandoned

He was here all along

He is the silent stillness

In silence does He dwell

He speaks in gentle whispers

Reminds me all is well

So should the silent stillness

Come knocking at my door

I'll open for Him gladly

And this I know for sure

I'd Never Box A Kangaroo

I'd never box a kangaroo,

Nor swim with crocodiles,

I'd not feast with sandy dingos,

No, not even if they smiled.

Why don't you come and box with me?

Asks the smirking kangaroo.

I'll let you win, I promise,

Let's go a round or two!

How would you like to come and swim?

Says the grinning crocodile.

It's cool in here, and hot out there,

Why don't you stay a while?

Come feast with us, oh won't you please?

The laughing dingos beg.

We've set a place right here for you,

Come now, shake a leg.

Oh no, I'd say. Forget it!

None of you fool me.

I know exactly what you want,

I'll stay well clear, you'll see!

I'd never box a kangaroo,

Nor swim with crocodiles,

I'd not feast with sandy dingos,

No, not even if they smiled.

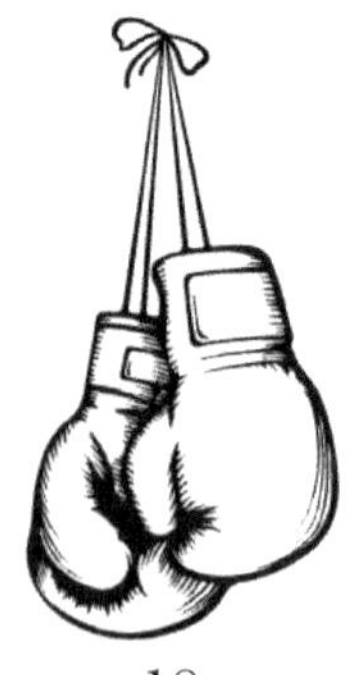

Soft Moonbeams Shimmer

Soft moonbeams shimmer in the night,

When silver stars are all aglow.

Now sun is gone, all tucked up tight,

Soft moonbeams shimmer in the night.

Bright meteors, oh, what a sight!

And the wise planets surely know,

Soft moonbeams shimmer in the night,

When silver stars are all aglow.

Ode to the Unknown Soldier

I know the flag you fought for,
But I've never heard your name.
I know the land you left behind,
But not who waited here in vain.

I've heard the people speak of you,
In hushed and whispered tones.
I've seen them bow their heads and say,
'Mate, you've made it home.'

I've stepped into the marble hall,
Your gilded tomb of gold.
And wondered quietly to myself,
Why does it feel so cold?

I've seen the place you used to rest,
In that land so far, far flung.

I've walked the trench where you once sat,

Where the bloodstained banners hung.

I do not know your name, my friend,

Though I've been where you have been.

But I'd not like to rest alone,

Had I seen what you had seen.

So I'm sorry that they came one day,

And disturbed your resting bones.

I'm sorry that they dragged you back,

And said they'd brought you home.

Your mates aren't here, the ones you loved,

The men you fought beside.

Those who you called your brothers,

With whom you hoped and prayed and died.

And if anyone who knew you once,

Happened upon your tomb,

They'd never know that here you lay,

Within this golden room.

And so it is with sadness,

That I write these words today.

This was a man who fought for us,

And who we then betrayed.

Because did we ever think,

That when we raised his bones,

Whether he might want to stay,

With his mates beneath their stones?

But guilty hearts will justify,

This cruel and heinous crime.

To take a dead man from his grave,

And suspend him within time.

To point and say, we brought him back,

There's no blood upon our hands!

We're not the ones who sent him there,

To die in foreign lands!

But I'll put the question to you,

If your hands are truly clean,

Why feel the need to point at all,

When to remember's all you need?

With Wild Thunderstorms

I've run with wild thunderstorms

And cast a spell under the moon

I've gone against the well-worn norm

I've run with wild thunderstorms

With ancient gods I've played old tunes

I've run with wild thunderstorms

And cast a spell under the moon

Sir Lancelot saw Guinevere

Sir Lancelot saw Guinevere

While dancing in King Arthur's hall

Spinning under the chandelier

Her saintly gaze held him in thrall

Under glittering crystal stars

Sir Lancelot saw Guinevere

She caged his heart in golden bars

Although she had not yet come near

Old Camelot trembled for fear

For those walls knew their time had come

Sir Lancelot saw Guinevere

Now all Britain would be undone

When Arthur's work was laid to waste

Bold men would cross themselves in fear

When they heard how, under her lace

Sir Lancelot saw Guinevere

The Weeping Willow

Why does the weeping willow cry

Which of her plans have gone awry

Why does she stand all day and weep

What awful secrets does she keep

Grief of widows, bent and broken

Dreams of lovers never spoken

Is this why she laments so deep

What awful secrets does she keep

Children's thoughts now long forgotten

Plans of bridegrooms' misbegotten

Tears falling for she never sleeps

What awful secrets does she keep

Why does the weeping willow cry

What awful secrets does she keep

The Sea's Exhale

The wine dark sea doth never sleep,

And many secrets does she keep.

In her embrace young sailors rest,

Their ships sunken in her sand.

Pillowed against her cold, grey breast,

They dream of lives once lived on land.

Widowed wives, they weep and wail,

The waves just give a soft exhale.

The wine dark sea doth never sleep,

And many secrets does she keep.

Oh, she could sing in gentle verse,

Of creatures humans have not seen.

Of treasure gold, a sea god's curse,

Terrible monsters that have been.

But she will not speak her tale,

The waves just give a soft exhale.

The wine dark sea doth never sleep,

And many secrets does she keep.

Who Stood Here

A whispered myth became a shout

A wishful falsehood drowned truth out

We went to war, never returned

Our sacrifice of no concern

We would have told, you listened not

Discarded truths your dead begot

So tell your lies, your gilded glories

We know the truth, you stole our stories

Then speak fervently if you dare

The myths of heroism there

Though here we stood, and here we fell

It isn't our truths that you tell

Though here we be in foreign ground

We shall not sleep while lies abound

The Graveyard

Walking slowly by the stones that mark,

The places where lie broken hearts.

A breath of wind dare not disturb

Those resting here all unobserved.

A mournful, warbling magpie cries,

Before, in grief, she takes to the skies.

She leaves behind this cold, grey world,

Of stone and earth and dreams all furled.

I'll linger a little longer here,

Thoughts and day both crisp and clear.

Before I leave in place of death,

And trade it in for life's sweet breath.

Darwinisim

I wonder if Charles Darwin thought

That a day like this would come

When we'd tailor evolution

Like we make our wine and rum

And if he'd stopped and paused to think

That dear old Charlie darling

Would he have been so keen to share

His scientific rambling

For there's no end to what we'll do

(Adolf Hitler would approve!)

Blue eyes, blonde hair, a freckled nose

This and more we can now choose

And if a defect there may be

Some unwanted natural glitch

Backspace, edit, and out it goes

With barely a single hitch

But is it right for us to say
What makes a life worth living
To edit generations come
Before they've started giving

And is in an honest science
Or a truly depraved game
Darwinism for the future
Genocide without that name

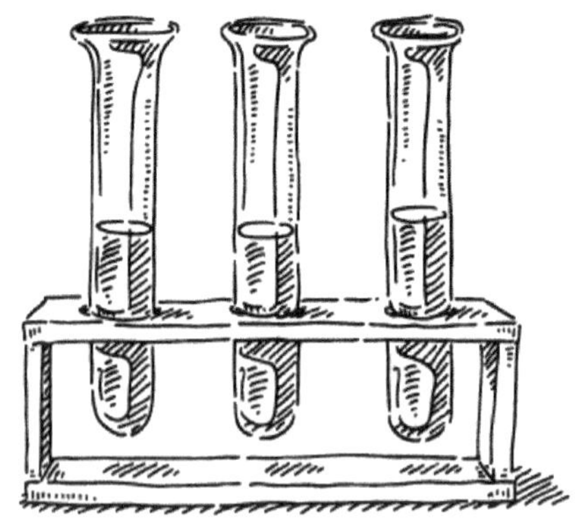

www.ingramcontent.com/pod-product-compliance
Lightning Source LLC
LaVergne TN
LVHW051241200726
843510LV00011B/1648